WORKBOOK

for

FINANCIAL FEMINIST

Overcome the Patriarchy's Bullsh*t to Master Your Money and Build a Life You Love

Morales Press

DISCLAIMER

This workbook is intended to complement and supplement the information provided in the main book. It is important to note that this workbook is not intended to replace the original book. Instead, it is designed to enhance the reader's understanding and application of the concepts presented in the original work.

This Book Belong to....

Table of content

INTRODUCTION

This extensive workbook was created as a result of a personal journey greatly impacted by the disclosures found in financial feminist literature. A moving narrative about a woman negotiating the difficulties of money talks and liberating herself through exposing her vulnerabilities lodged itself in my mind while I read the main book. The necessity for a practical supplement to the theoretical insights presented in the main book became evident after this moving experience.

The workbook fills the obvious gap between theory and practice; it is a labor of love. Observing the woman's freedom highlighted how urgent it is to translate financial feminist ideas into useful, accessible instruments. This workbook is a promise to empower people who, like her, long for a concrete road map to financial independence, not merely a response to that desire. This workbook transforms complex financial ideas into manageable steps, making it a valuable resource for anybody looking to go from financial dependency to empowerment.

This workbook captures the essence of financial feminism and makes it a personal and approachable experience with exercises, relatable anecdotes, and thought-provoking suggestions. It is an invitation to explore the many levels of financial complexity, question social norms, and set out on a journey towards long-term economic empowerment, rather than just a guide. Let's explore the intricacies of financial freedom together and incorporate our own stories into the larger picture of the revolutionary potential of financial   feminism.

HOW TO MAKE USE OF THIS WORKBOOK

Embark on your financial feminist journey with this workbook. Start by delving into your emotions, mindset, and childhood impact on money. You can align your relationship and money goals with the help of this workbook detailed approach. Handle moral spending, get involved in advocacy, and have candid conversations with friends about money. Incorporate politics into your choices and make a long-term financial strategy your priority. Let every segment serve as a first step towards achieving both financial and societal transformation. Your road map to long-term financial security and significant influence is provided by this guide.

Chapter 1: The Emotions of Money

Detailed Chapter Summary

Expert in finances Kristine highlights the value of delving emotionally into financial issues and figuring out where they stem from. Financial decisions are psychological in nature, shaped by our attitudes and emotions. Financial decisions are heavily influenced by emotions, and making wise judgments requires an awareness of the relationship between emotions and finances. Anxiety-based emotions like shame can drive people to conformity and perfection, which keeps them from strengthening their financial foundation. People are prevented from achieving financial literacy, stability, and confidence by the Five Patriarchal Narratives, which are structured by patriarchal views. People can have a strong relationship with money and use more of it to provide happiness, security, and solace by comprehending the causes of shame and converting it into rage.

The notion that hard effort brings riches and success is maintained by the American Dream narrative, which has its roots in racism and is promoted by financial experts. Men and women are both frequently portrayed in this narrative as being kind and selfless, which frequently causes feelings of guilt and shame. The goal of financial feminism is to subvert gender norms held by men and force the wealthiest to consider their existence as a means of serving others. We can endeavor to improve the world by bridging the gap in inequality and guaranteeing underprivileged people have alternatives. Gaining insight into one's financial views can aid people in managing their spending and achieving their objectives.

Financial flashpoint experiences, financial status, and financial alertness all have a big impact on our attitudes and actions. Money scripts that predict financial behaviors might be created as a result of childhood financial crisis experiences and socioeconomic background. Long-term effects of historical and generational trauma could include a distrust of institutions and a dread of being taken advantage of once more. It is critical to establish a link between our first financial memories and our current financial basis if we are to alter our connection with money. Clients who attend financial coaching sessions can examine their financial issues and learn how to make better decisions. Changing our perspective entails letting go of guilt and condemnation, putting the present first, and conquering unfavorable money-related ideas. Having enough money can provide people happiness, self-assurance, and freedom of choice, enabling them to interact with others and the world in new ways. We may design a more rewarding existence by adopting new financial concepts and mindsets.

Key Lesson

Emotions are a major factor in financial decision-making; they affect everything from investment selections to spending patterns. For long-lasting financial transformation, it is imperative to recognize and treat the emotional component of money. A foundation for knowledgeable decision-making and financial assurance is laid by emotionally deconstructing financial problems and figuring out their underlying causes.

Expert Advice and Guidance

Financial expert Kristine stresses the importance of emotionally decompressing before offering practical financial guidance. The chapter emphasizes the negative effects of social narratives and guilt on one's ability to manage finances. The financial psychologist Dr. Brad Klontz provides insightful information on past trauma, money views, and the impact of early events. These insights can be very helpful for overcoming financial obstacles.

Interactive Self Reflective Question

Go back to your earliest financial recollection. How can this memory be affecting your thinking and financial choices now?

_____

_____

_____

_____

_____

_____

_____

_____

_____

_____

_____

_____

_____

_____

_____

Examine the cultural narratives surrounding gender roles and money to counter patriarchal ones. What effects have these stories had on your willingness to have frank conversations about money and how successful you think you are financially?

_____

_____

_____

_____

_____

_____

_____

_____

_____

_____

_____

_____

_____

_____

_____

_____

_____

Take into account the four categories of money that Dr. Klontz has identified: money avoidance, money worship, money status, and money vigilance. How do these attitudes affect the way you handle money?

_____

_____

_____

_____

_____

_____

_____

_____

_____

_____

_____

_____

_____

_____

_____

_____

_____

Imagine living a better life where your relationship with money has improved. What options and experiences would open up? How may having a stable financial situation affect your general wellbeing?

_____

_____

_____

_____

_____

_____

_____

_____

_____

_____

_____

_____

_____

_____

_____

Chapter 2: Spending

Detailed Chapter Summary

The author talks about the misogyny in financial advice for women, with a particular emphasis on the misogyny in women's spending and the spending habits of men. According to their argument, two thirds of financial advice aimed at women labels them as excessive spenders, and 90% of it concentrates on money-saving tips. The author contends that discretionary spending—which is not always a free choice—is frequently dismissed by the patriarchy as trivial. Black women in particular are frequently chastised for their textured hair and grooming-related expenditures. Critics claim that women pay more for equivalent goods and services, a practice known as the "pink tax." The author makes a point of saying that it's okay to spend money on necessities or wants. She contends that since everyone spends, all money saved will ultimately be used for retirement savings, down payments, and emergencies.

Although money can be a great instrument for creating a life we enjoy, it should only be used for deliberate purchases that support our beliefs and areas of interest. Determining our desires and making deliberate purchases that are in line with our interests and values are essential to living a Rich Life. Living a Rich Life is putting more of an emphasis on happiness, exploration, and giving than on structural problems. Achieving a Rich Life requires figuring out how much money really matters to you, finding a balance between goals and spending, and beginning to spend with awareness. The Money Diary is one tool that may be used to track purchases and identify trends. By keeping a money journal, you can spot trends in your spending and assess your expenditures objectively rather than criticizing your own spending choices. As an outsider assessing expenditure, you might position yourself for future success.

The author recommends reassessing purchases and emphasizing value-based spending in order to make better financial decisions and increase pleasure. By thinking back on your Three Value Categories, you'll be able to pinpoint your joys and more freely spend your money in those areas. Another crucial concept is Afford Anything, which holds that every dollar spent must be offset by savings on other expenses. Value-based spending enables you to distribute scarce resources according to your priorities. Emotions and mental states might impact one's inclination toward emotional spending, thus it's important to weigh an item's worth in relation to its possible applications. It is important to think about whether or not you are voting with your money when making financial decisions.

Key Lesson

Misogynistic financial advice for women has a history of fostering negative stereotypes and ignoring the particular difficulties encountered by those on the margins. The chapter questions established myths and highlights the significance of changing the way that people talk about money, dealing with structural problems, and giving women the power to make deliberate decisions.

Expert Advice and Guidance

The author questions conventional wisdom about money, which frequently holds women responsible for their inability to accumulate riches by frivolous spending. They support a values-based approach to purchasing, in which people match their goals and interests with the things they want to buy. This chapter examines how emotions influence financial decisions and presents resources such as the Money Diary.

Interactive Self Reflective Question

Determine which aspects of your life are most fulfilling and consistent with your values. For more enjoyment, think about devoting a larger portion of your budget to these areas.

_____

_____

_____

_____

_____

_____

_____

_____

_____

_____

_____

_____

_____

_____

_____

Consider your feelings and mental state before making a buy. Consider whether the purchase will make a significant and long-lasting difference in your life, or if it is motivated by the desire to cope emotionally.

_____

_____

_____

_____

_____

_____

_____

_____

_____

_____

_____

_____

_____

_____

_____

_____

Determine an item's value by determining how it might be used in the world. Examine the item's value in relation to its cost, taking into account aspects like quality and whether it's on sale.

_____

_____

_____

_____

_____

_____

_____

_____

_____

_____

_____

_____

_____

_____

_____

Consider the effects of the purchases you make. To ensure that your purchases reflect your values, think about patronizing local businesses, businesses owned by people of color, or businesses owned by women.

_____

_____

_____

_____

_____

_____

_____

_____

_____

_____

_____

_____

_____

_____

_____

Chapter 3: The Financial Game Plan

Detailed Chapter Summary

One of the main reasons why so many individuals struggle with money is the Ostrich Effect, a cognitive bias brought on by embarrassment and discomfort when evaluating personal finances. Knowing our financial objectives and concentrating on saving for when and where we want to travel are crucial for maintaining financial control. Due of historical prejudices against women and unseen scripts like the American Dream and the notion that attending college is a waste of money, understanding financial ownership is essential.

It is imperative that we develop a step-by-step plan and a Why for our goals in order to transform our relationship with money. You will feel more accomplished and be on track to meet your financial objectives if you set clear, attainable, and mission-driven goals. The Financial Game Plan is a tool that helps people manage their money better by helping them define timely, precise, and goal-driven objectives for different financial circumstances.

Regardless of debt, age, income, or financial objectives, everyone can benefit from using the Financial Priority List as a step-by-step road map for their whole financial future. Recovering required expenses is priority zero since improving one's financial situation necessitates looking after oneself.

In conclusion, the Financial Game Plan is a tool that helps people manage their money wisely by establishing clear, attainable, and motivational goals. Keeping three to six months' worth of living expenses stashed away in a high-yield savings account (HYSA) is another recommendation to avoid accruing further debt in the process of trying to pay for an emergency. In times of crisis, prioritizing one's well-being and concentrating on financial objectives can be achieved by safeguarding one's health and paying off high-interest debt.

Determining high-interest debt, retirement investment, and lower-interest debt repayment are financial priorities. The best way to optimize stock market returns is to pay off higher-interest debt before lower-interest debt. Investing for retirement has the potential to yield a higher rate of return than debt with lower interest rates. Large-ticket items should be saved in addition to retirement investments and debt repayment with lower interest rates. Prior to beginning debt repayment, make sure you contribute enough to reach the employer match on retirement accounts such as 401(k) or 403(b) if your employer matches contributions.

The Financial Game Plan places a strong emphasis on budgeting since it enables people to spend their money on the things they enjoy, guilt-free. People can enjoy their financial journey and escape the guilt of not taking care of their finances by adhering to the Financial Game Plan.

The 3 Bucket Budget is a nonbudget budgeting method that permits guilt-free spending while placing a higher priority on financial and personal well-being. There are three categories in it: aims, enjoyable categories, and essential expenses. The author talks about bucketizing money and how automating, automating, automating may revolutionize it.

There is no one-size-fits-all strategy for saving money every month because personal finance is a personal experience. Putting money into three categories—50% for expenses, 20% for objectives, and

30% for leisure—is a smart place to start. Put limits on each bucket and monitor more specific spending if your revenue is erratic.

Key Lesson

The Ostrich Effect, which is defined as putting off or ignoring financial issues out of discomfort, is a significant barrier to wise money management. Recognizing financial realities, establishing specific goals, and comprehending the motivation behind them are all necessary to overcome this bias.

Expert Advice and Guidance

- Face Financial Reality: Although facing financial difficulties can be difficult, putting off doing so will only make the issue worse. Begin by evaluating your financial status objectively and honestly.
- Have Meaningful Goals: It's important to have financial objectives that align with your values and ambitions. Having a specific goal in mind, such as saving for a dream home, a trip, or an emergency fund, makes money management more interesting and doable.
- Financial Ownership: Historically, prejudices have made it difficult for people to own their finances, particularly for women. Realize how freeing and empowering it is to take charge of your finances. Being financially responsible is not a burden, but a means to freedom.
- Difficulty Invisible Scripts: Contest popular narratives such as the American Dream or college-related assumptions. Change your perspective to one of abundance by defining success and financial well-being according to your own principles rather than those of society.

Interactive Self Reflective Question

Which financial aspects are you uncomfortable talking about? How may recognizing and resolving these issues result in constructive change?

_____

_____

_____

_____

_____

_____

_____

_____

_____

_____

_____

_____

_____

_____

Identify Your Financial Why is improvement in finances essential to you? What are your long-term objectives, and how may they guide and inspire you on your financial path?

_____

_____

_____

_____

_____

_____

_____

_____

_____

_____

_____

_____

_____

_____

_____

_____

Do you feel that unseen scripts or societal attitudes are influencing the way you make financial decisions? In what ways could questioning these presumptions result in a more purposeful and happy financial life?

_____

_____

_____

_____

_____

_____

_____

_____

_____

_____

_____

_____

_____

_____

_____

_____

See yourself in a situation where you have reached your financial objectives. In what ways does this vision correspond with your principles, and what actions can you take right now to make it a reality?

_____

_____

_____

_____

_____

_____

_____

_____

_____

_____

_____

_____

_____

_____

_____

Chapter 4: Debt

Detailed Chapter Summary

The exorbitant expense of college tuition and common misconceptions about debt, which has always played a significant role in our economy, are topics covered by the author. Being in debt does not imply a lack of worth or shame because it is not a personal flaw. Debt is something that many people must have, and that should not be reason for shame. Credit card firms frequently use deception to trick potential clients into applying without fully comprehending the rules of the card, which can result in discrimination and lawsuits.

The false belief that debt is always bad and should be avoided at all costs is another topic covered by the author. When possessed by wealthy individuals, debt is not referred to be debt but rather leverage. Richer people are typically rewarded for making wise business decisions by taking on debt. We have to tackle debt head-on if we want to win the game.

The author concludes by highlighting how critical it is to recognize and dispel common misconceptions regarding debt and how it affects one's financial stability. We may move toward a more just and equitable society by realizing the effects of debt and the part played by white supremacist.

Living debt-free is a personal achievement and a means of subverting patriarchal institutions. But it takes diligence, perseverance, and regularity. When you borrow money and have to pay it back, you are said to be in debt. The principal is the amount you originally borrowed, and interest and a portion of the principal balance are paid each month. You keep owing more than you originally agreed to, which makes compounding debt dangerous.

When paying off debt, one must weigh the principle against the interest, with high-interest debt being more costly than investing. It could be challenging for you to make principal payments because lenders profit more the longer you are in debt. It's crucial to contribute more money to the loan's principle sum in order to pay off debt sooner.

Some people employ methods to make their debt vanish without thinking through the repercussions or making a strategy to pay it off. Balance transfers, 0% interest loans, and debt consolidation are the Holy Trinity of debt quick fixes. However, they are potentially dangerous options that only come into play when the numbers add up and you have a plan in place to pay off your debt.

To pay off debt, compare interest rates, arrange debt according to interest rate and remaining balance, and establish an emergency fund to cover your expenses in case of an unforeseen circumstance.

Reducing high-interest debt is essential, but if you have several debts that are more than 7% APR, go for the Bank of America card with the smaller balance as the lower-hanging fruit. Make the best decision for you because personal finance matters. Asking inquiries about interest rates, loan conditions, and the ethics, reputation, and customer service of your creditor is a responsible way to take on debt. There is no magic wand that will make all debt go away, therefore when making this decision, trust your instinct.

Personal and financial lives can be greatly impacted by loans, however credit card debt should be avoided since it can negatively affect your financial situation. While credit cards can be used sensibly, it's important to pay your bills on schedule and refrain from using your credit cards to carry a balance. A credit score of

750 is considered perfect, although anything beyond that is regarded as "good" credit.

Paying your bills on time and avoiding credit card debt are vital for maintaining a good credit score, which is an important aspect of personal finance. Experts recommend keeping your credit score below 30% in order to establish a strong credit history. You can reduce your credit utilization rate by taking advantage of your credit line and not utilizing it.

When applying for new credit, one of the greatest methods to manage your money is to check your credit score. You may also avoid hard credit queries by doing this. Taking charge of your credit score is one of the finest methods to improve your financial mobility, possibly for future generations as well as for yourself.

Key Lesson

One intricate and varied component of personal finance that is entwined with prejudices and cultural systems is debt. To make wise financial decisions, one must comprehend the complexities of debt, its effects on specific people, and the wider economic ramifications.

Expert Advice and Guidance

- Debunking Common Myths About Debt: Not all debt is made equal. It's critical to distinguish between predatory debt, which has outrageous interest rates and abusive behaviors, and fair debt, which promotes attainment of milestones and personal development.
- In Navigating Patriarchal Systems, the author emphasizes how patriarchal systems have a disproportionate impact on women when it comes to debt. Individuals are empowered to confront and overcome systemic prejudices when they

are aware of these dynamics and make wise financial decisions.

- Managing Debt Reduction Strategically: Paying off high-interest debt should come first because it can be more costly than investing. Make a well-organized plan by using debt payback calculators. The length of debt repayment can be considerably impacted by making strategic payments toward the principal sum.

Management of Credit Scores: Financial mobility depends on having a high credit score. Recognize that credit utilization, on-time payments, and credit history are among the criteria that affect credit ratings. It is advantageous to check your credit score on a regular basis, and it has no bad effects. Proactively seek credit line increases and steer clear of hard credit inquiries to raise your credit score.

Interactive Self Reflective Question

Think about situations like home ownership or educational investments where going on debt could be a wise move. What role does prudent debt management have in one's financial and personal development?

_____

_____

_____

_____

_____

_____

_____

_____

_____

_____

_____

_____

_____

_____

_____

Consider the biases that exist in the financial systems. What possible effects can patriarchal institutions in society have on your ability to obtain loans and make financial decisions?

_____

_____

_____

_____

_____

_____

_____

_____

_____

_____

_____

_____

_____

_____

_____

Consider any feelings of guilt or low self-esteem that may be connected to debt. How can a more positive financial mindset be achieved by carefully managing debt and redefining it as a tool for growth?

_____
_____
_____
_____
_____
_____
_____
_____
_____
_____
_____
_____
_____
_____
_____
_____
_____
_____

How can knowing and actively controlling your credit score help you have more financial mobility? What potential effects can this understanding have on your capacity to handle important life events and seize improved financial opportunities?

_____

_____

_____

_____

_____

_____

_____

_____

_____

_____

_____

_____

_____

_____

_____

Chapter 5: Investing

Often disregarded as a sexist icon, the Wall Street Bull represents advancement in finance. Due to the fact that women frequently delay investing longer than males, there is a wealth gap that restricts their alternatives and way of life. Black women have a low median wealth of $1,700, while Hispanic women have a poor median wealth of $1,000. These are significantly worse figures for women of color. Because of these investing and wealth disparities, women over 65 are more likely to be impoverished.

Another factor preventing women from investing more is the salary divide; women make less money than males, which makes it more difficult for them to succeed in the stock market. Women save more of their wages than males do, according to an analysis by Fidelity Investments, but they save less overall in terms of money. Even among those who can afford to invest, only 28% of women say they feel comfortable doing so.

With only 15% of Wall Street traders and 23% of financial advisors being women, financial advice, and especially investing advice, has historically been dominated by white men. Certain misconceptions prevent people from feeling comfortable investing: saving money; investment is risky; and you should wait till you have more money.

In summary, investing is about making steady, steady, and long-term financial decisions over time rather than gambling or trying to get rich overnight.

In addition to gaining financial power and bridging the wealth gap, investing is essential for women who hope to retire and stop working in the future. Women often outlive men by seven years, making retirement the most expensive expense of your life. Make investments in tax-advantaged retirement accounts, such 401(k)s or IRAs, to start saving for retirement. A maximum annual contribution of $20,500 can be made by individuals into tax-advantaged traditional and Roth accounts.

It is imperative that women invest for their futures and learn from the mistakes of others. Investing is a sophisticated skill that everyone can learn and hone. You can purchase stocks and bonds, which are the two primary goods. Bonds are the debt of a corporation or the government, whereas stocks are little pieces of companies. Investing in stocks is advised by financial advisors when you are younger (often under forty to forty-five years old), when you can afford to be more aggressive.

To make sure you're well-diversified, investing entails making intelligent investment selections and diversifying your portfolio. Your portfolio can be made more diverse by using mutual funds, exchange-traded funds (ETFs), target-date funds, and index funds. Selecting stocks and bonds on your own, or through services like Fidelity, Vanguard, and Charles Schwab, is known as DIY investing. By requesting information about goals, retirement dates, and risk tolerance, robo-advisors can automate investing. However, they can be costly and do not provide process explanations or investment education.

Avoid consuming too much information about the stock market and concentrate on making well-informed investment selections that you are comfortable with. To assist you in making well-informed financial decisions, Treasury provides an accessible manner. Compared to index funds, which usually have fees of less than 0.2%, actively managed funds, such target-date funds, can have higher fees. Making ensuring your portfolio is well-diversified and not concentrated in a single firm or sector is crucial.

Start investing or up your contribution to ensure that you are making well-informed decisions. Each day that you do not invest is a day that you are losing out on. Recall that the investment process is lengthy, and unless you sell your investments, you have not lost money even in a down market for stocks.

Given that her student loan debt is less than 7% of average stock market return, Jessica should concentrate on making maximum contributions to her 401(k) or IRA in the Financial Game Plan. When she hits her limit on one, she ought to begin making contributions to the other. It's a common misperception that everybody who becomes a millionaire can retire. You are the only one who knows your retirement number, and you can reach it with your returns.

Certified financial planner Tim Nash, the founder of Good Investment, discusses her path to financial independence (FI) and the significance of understanding that retirement is a continuum that is subject to change. Rather than spreading it out throughout the entire year, she advocates pursuing seasonal jobs and concentrating on income-generating opportunities.

The most effective way to increase wealth is by investing, so even if you only have a small amount of money to start with, it's important to be deliberate about selecting the best platform.

Key Lesson

Women frequently encounter obstacles and misunderstandings that prevent them from investing, despite the fact that it's a vital tool for accumulating wealth and reaching financial independence. It is necessary to dispel fallacies, comprehend investing possibilities, and acknowledge the value of purposeful and moral investing in order to get past these obstacles.

- Closing the Gender Wealth disparity: The author highlights that there is a wealth disparity that affects women of color in particular. One method to address this issue and provide a route to retirement security and financial empowerment is through investing.

- Tackling Myths: A number of false beliefs around investing are addressed, including the notion that it is always dangerous or that conserving money is adequate on its own. Women are encouraged by the professional advice to view investment as a long-term, steady approach as opposed to a high-risk bet.

- Diversity and Inclusion in Investing: The author recognizes that historically, white men have dominated the financial advisory industry and emphasizes the significance of changing this. We can work toward a more inclusive future by supporting equal treatment in financial advice services and encouraging women to get involved in investing.

Ethical and Responsible Investing: This chapter discusses impact and socially responsible investing as means of coordinating financial objectives with individual values. Women's investments can contribute to a more sustainable and fair world by staying away from industries that hurt society and by supporting businesses that promote positive social change.

Interactive Self Reflective Question

Think about the wealth figures that are shown for women and women of color. What role may investing play in addressing structural wealth inequities and providing a vehicle for personal financial growth? How might deliberate investing help achieve financial parity?

_____

_____

_____

_____

_____

_____

_____

_____

_____

_____

_____

_____

_____

_____

_____

Examine your own attitudes about investing and any possible fears you may have. In what way may realizing that fear is a taught behavior be empowering? Think back to any personal encounters or cultural messaging that might have shaped your investment confidence or reluctance.

_____

_____

_____

_____

_____

_____

_____

_____

_____

_____

_____

_____

_____

_____

_____

_____

_____

The author recommends diversification as a crucial tactic. In what ways does diversification help with risk management in an investing portfolio? Take into account your own risk tolerance and financial objectives as you assess the advantages and difficulties of diversification.

_____

_____

_____

_____

_____

_____

_____

_____

_____

_____

_____

_____

_____

_____

_____

_____

_____

_____

Assess the idea and consequences of socially conscious investing. How do financial objectives fit with personal values? Think about the possible trade-offs and if you would give ethical issues a higher priority when making investment decisions.

_____

_____

_____

_____

_____

_____

_____

_____

_____

_____

_____

_____

_____

_____

_____

_____

Chapter 6: Earning

Detailed Chapter Summary

Financial expert Tori struggled with underpaying and rejection anxiety at a Fortune 500 company. She also experienced a toxic work atmosphere. At nine years old, she launched her first business. She went on to pursue other ventures, including social media management, freelance writing, and a blog for women in their twenties. In the realm of finance, the average salary difference between men and women is large, with women earning 82 cents for every $1 earned by males. To solve this problem, financial feminism has to concentrate on systemic and policy change. The author talks about her personal experience of changing careers and discovering a new sense of purpose after working long hours in a toxic workplace. Achieving financial success does not include engaging in a hustle culture or confusing wealth with value. A job that suits one's lifestyle should be paid reasonably and treated kindly by the employer, business, and customers.

This chapter addresses common misunderstandings about full-time employment, freelancing, and starting a business that impede one's ability to change careers and increase income. Career change can be impeded by a variety of variables, not just hard effort, devotion, and fear of failure. The pressure from society to fit in can cause poisoning and the idea that one's existing circumstances are all that one deserves. The counsel given to women in the professional workforce lacks intersectionality, despite the fact that passion and money are not mutually exclusive. In sharing their experiences, the author highlights the value of having a strong work ethic, a mentor, and appropriate boundaries when overcoming obstacles in landing a job and negotiating a salary. Being honest with oneself about what occurs if they don't ask for what they want is crucial, and learning to bargain is critical to growing revenue throughout one's career.

For wage negotiations to be effective, the author stresses how crucial it is to know your market rate and value-add. Your market rate may be more accurately represented by using personal experiences and data from other platforms. Get input from peers and use narrative to highlight your achievements in order to highlight your value-add. Women must bargain for better pay since underpricing might result from not negotiating. This is especially true in the workplace. Start with a large number and concentrate on personal development to prevent underpricing. Instead of being motivated by conflict, negotiations should be cooperative. It is best to ask for a greater number than what you would be willing to accept rather than the one you want. Well-being is given priority and a healthy environment is fostered by this strategy.

In order to decide if a firm is the correct fit for you, you must first learn about its beliefs, leaders, and operations before engaging in negotiations. When starting a side business, it's important to take value, talent, and time commitment into account. Your willingness to commit time is a function of both your available time and your willingness to make time. Value is the amount you need or desire to be earning, while talent is the set of talents you may utilize to obtain additional revenue. Starting from scratch can be more profitable than taking up part-time work, but it requires persistence and patience. A devoted spouse and time-separation skills are essential components of a strong support network for a side gig to succeed. Build one revenue source at a time and expand your options step by step to create many revenue streams. In order to address systemic problems and the absence of egalitarian policies, discrimination based on income is essential. Better mental health, the development of jobs, and general well-being can result from creating possibilities to better the lives of you and your coworkers.

Key Lesson

Redefining Success beyond Traditional Norms

Success doesn't have to follow conventional norms, as Tori's experience shows us. Her experiences with different professional paths and toxic environments emphasize how important it is to redefine success on our own terms, prioritizing our own well-being, passion, and sense of fulfillment over social expectations.

Expert Advice and Guidance

Embrace Entrepreneurship and Diverse Income Streams

Entrepreneurial Spirit: The importance of fostering an entrepreneurial spirit is highlighted by Tori's early-stage entrepreneurial experience. To succeed, acknowledge your special abilities, make a strong impression on others, and be willing to consider different options.

Diversify Your Sources of Income: Tori's move from a nasty 9-to-5 job to freelancing and blogging highlights the need of doing just that. To achieve financial stability and flexibility, take into account a variety of income sources, such as side gigs, investments, or freelance work.

Interactive Self Reflective Question

Evaluate if your concept of success conforms to the standards of success that society has established. What new meaning can you give to success so that it aligns more with your goals and values?

_____
_____
_____
_____
_____
_____
_____
_____
_____
_____
_____
_____
_____
_____
_____
_____
_____

What abilities or interests can you use for a side gig or small business if Tori's story of entrepreneurship speaks to you? In what ways could this enhance your sense of well-being in general?

_____

_____

_____

_____

_____

_____

_____

_____

_____

_____

_____

_____

_____

_____

_____

_____

_____

Consider your sources of revenue at the moment. Exist prospects for diversification that would guarantee a more stable financial future? What other endeavors or abilities may you pursue to generate extra revenue streams?

_____

_____

_____

_____

_____

_____

_____

_____

_____

_____

_____

_____

_____

_____

_____

_____

Sadly, many people can identify with Tori's experiences in toxic work environments. In what ways can you put your health first at work or look for other settings that better reflect your beliefs?

_____

_____

_____

_____

_____

_____

_____

_____

_____

_____

_____

_____

_____

_____

_____

_____

_____

Chapter 7: Living a Financial Feminist Lifestyle

Detailed Chapter Summary

The significance of comprehending emotions, attitude, and childhood influences on financial management, budgeting, thoughtful purchasing decisions, and stock market investing is emphasized throughout the text. It also talks about how the economic system depends on inequality and how important it is to provide for others financially. Only when one prioritizes their own needs does financial feminism work. Setting aside money for one's own needs is essential because doing so can lead to resentment and tension. Effective money management and maintaining a healthy lifestyle can be achieved with the support of sustainable financial self-care techniques like meditation, eating a balanced diet, and setting limits. In addition to sharing their own financial self-care and open communication practices, the author discusses their personal problems with kitchen cleaning and their Money Date ritual.

With the help of Money Date, kids can manage their money and plan forward for the future with knowledge. It include inspecting purchases to make sure they match financial and lifestyle goals, reporting fraud, examining spending, and locating unused subscriptions. When setting financial goals, like opening an emergency fund or making contributions to a retirement account, the Money Date is a good time to review your progress. Prioritizing financial responsibilities and thinking back on objectives and their justifications are crucial. The Money Date must be nonnegotiable, occurring once a month, or more frequently if needed, and it must be set on a Sunday night. It is something that should be done for the rest of one's life and calls for grace and patience. Savings should be the first source of an emergency fund in case of need.

Social considerations and individual financial objectives make it difficult to maintain financial stability in today's environment. It can be beneficial to relationships and accountability to share financial experiences with friends and accountability partners. By seeing money as a tool for choice and living the life one desires, the author promotes normalizing the conversation around money. Closing the inequality gap requires acknowledging privilege and resisting injustice. For financial stability, ethical purchase choices are crucial, such as steering clear of busy shopping seasons. In order to make more moral purchasing decisions that help the economy, the environment, and underpaid labor, companies should focus on profits while also taking into account women's influence over modest finances.

A shift in lifestyle entailing a dedication to principles and a framework is part of financial feminism. A sustainable strategy to spending can be established by beginning with a values exercise and formulating a financial mission statement. Avoiding unfavorable criticism can be facilitated by gathering steam and concentrating on safe and long-term enterprises. Change can be brought about by giving regularly to charitable causes and having candid conversations about money. Financial feminism requires understanding about money, institutional injustice, and the outside world in addition to creating a financial game plan. We can build a more sustainable future if we dedicate our entire lives to improving our own financial situation.

Key Lesson

Putting on your financial oxygen mask first is a metaphor that forms the core of the theme. Similar to airline safety warnings, it emphasizes how important it is to protect your financial security before helping others. Stress and resentment may result from sacrificing your financial security for the good of others. Set yourself first, balance your financial objectives with your personal development, and keep in mind that it's all about consistency more than perfection.

Expert Advice and Guidance

- Embrace Money Dates Into Your Routine: Andy Hill, a financial expert, advises turning money conversations into memorable and pleasurable Money Dates with your significant other. Now is the perfect moment to make plans, recognize successes, and match your financial situation to your ideal lifestyle.
- Teach Your Kids Financial Virtues: Take a methodical way to teaching your kids financial responsibility by learning from the author's experience. By rewarding chores with money and categorizing earnings, one can foster responsibility, values, and financial literacy.
- Contemplate via a Mini-Money Diary: Consider your financial choices objectively on a regular basis. With the help of a mini-money diary, you may look back on your purchases and gain insight into your spending habits and financial goals.

Cast Your Ethical Voting Wallet Vote: Recognize how your purchases will affect things. Think about making sustainable and moral decisions as a deliberate attempt to improve business processes.

Interactive Self Reflective Question

How can you make your money talks with your significant other into meaningful Money Dates? In your next conversation, share one financial objective.

_____

_____

_____

_____

_____

_____

_____

_____

_____

_____

_____

_____

_____

_____

_____

_____

Consider how your early life events
influenced the way you handle money today.
Decide which practices you wish to keep or
alter.

_____

_____

_____

_____

_____

_____

_____

_____

_____

_____

_____

_____

_____

_____

_____

_____

_____

_____

What minor adjustments to your shopping can you make to support the ethical wallet movement? How can your decisions improve business practices?

_____

_____

_____

_____

_____

_____

_____

_____

_____

_____

_____

_____

_____

_____

How can one live a daily financial feminist lifestyle? Think about doing little, manageable things to regularly incorporate empowerment into your life.

_____

_____

_____

_____

_____

_____

_____

_____

_____

_____

_____

_____

_____

_____

_____

_____

Conclusion

This workbook illuminates the transformative process of embracing financial feminism. The teachings emphasize the connection between financial decisions, thinking, and emotions. It becomes clear that putting oneself first is important, especially for women of color. It's like putting on your oxygen mask before trying to aid someone else. A practical way to match relationship development with financial objectives is to implement the "Money Date" technique. A larger story of good financial citizenship incorporates advocacy and ethical spending. Important lessons include having frank conversations about money with peers and normalizing these conversations. The interdependence of politics, finance, and personal decisions strengthens the influence that any person can have. The foundation of this all-encompassing strategy is developing a sustainable financial game plan. Your story of financial feminism is not over; rather, it is a continuous one, enhanced by fresh perspectives and poised to impact not only your own life but also the society in which you live.

Made in the USA
Las Vegas, NV
26 November 2024

12697236R00039